teacher's friend publications

Reproducible Pages for Early Learners!

M000111789

Little Kids... COUNT!

Counting Activities for Developing Beginning Math Skills!

Written and Illustrated by:
Karen Sevaly
Contributing Editor:
Libby Perez
Graphic Designer:
Cory Jackson

Look for All of Our Little Kids... Books at your local educational retailer!

Table of Contents

Copyright © 2000
Teacher's Friend, a Scholastic Company.
All rights reserved.
Printed in China.

ISBN-13 978-0-439-50411-9
ISBN-10 0-439-50411-2

Reproduction of these materials for commercial resale or distribution to an entire school or school district is strictly prohibited. Pages may be duplicated for one individual classroom set only. Material may not be reproduced for other purposes without the prior written permission of the publisher. For information regarding permission, write to Scholastic Teaching Resources, 557 Broadway, New York, NY, 10012.

Safety Warning! The activities and patterns in this book are appropriate for children ages 3 to 6 years old. It is important that children only use materials and products labeled child-safe and non-toxic. Remember that young children should always be supervised by a competent adult and youngsters must never be allowed to put small objects or art materials in their mouths. Please consult the manufacturer's safety warnings on all materials and equipment used with young children.

Little Kids... Books!

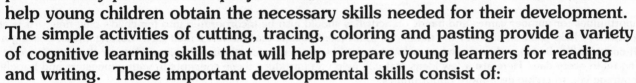

Welcome to the wonderful world of
young learners where play is learning
and learning is fun!

With these *Little Kids...Books!*, teachers can
provide easy patterns and projects that will
help young children obtain the necessary skills needed for their development.
The simple activities of cutting, tracing, coloring and pasting provide a variety
of cognitive learning skills that will help prepare young learners for reading
and writing. These important developmental skills consist of:

Fine Motor Skills
> finger-wrist dexterity, arm-hand movement, eye-hand coordination

Perceptual Motor Skills
> identification, color and shape recognition, matching and location,
> spatial relationships

Expressive and Receptive Language Skills
> listening, speaking, questioning, relating words and pictures,
> imitation, utilization, recognition and discrimination, visual
> perception and discrimination

Social and Emotional Skills
> creativity and imagination, pride in accomplishments, self-reliance,
> self-control, self-confidence

The early years of schooling helps determine how a child will learn for a life-
time. During this period, children develop a sense of self and decide whether
school is a burden or a joy. We hope these books assist you in your goal to
provide each child with a fulfilling and fun learning experience!

Introduction

Little Kids...Count!

Most young children begin expressing mathematical concepts as they discover the world around them. It is not uncommon for a child to say, "My truck is bigger than your truck," or, "I can jump higher than you." As the young learner progresses in awareness and cognitive skills through play, the concept of understanding and recognizing simple numbers should be introduced. The pages in this book provide a way in which you can introduce number recognition and counting 1-20. When using these worksheets, it is most important to encourage children to use manipulatives and everyday objects to demonstrate the number concepts being taught.

Note: Young children will need help reading the instructions on the worksheets in this book. Individually work with the child as he or she does each activity. After completing several worksheets, the child may be able to work more independently. However, make sure you give your attention to areas in which the child has most difficulty and always praise him or her for a job well done!

Opportunities for number games and hands-on activities should also be incorporated into the child's play time. It is also important to help children discover the numerous math relationships that make up their day. Sorting socks, pouring a half cup of milk, dialing a phone number or being in bed by a given time, all offer the young learner the experience of using math every day. Here are a few ideas that will help you introduce these concepts to your youngsters and hopefully encourage you to create even more opportunities.

COUNTING IDEAS:

Simple Counting - Have children line up small objects and count them. Cotton balls, peanuts, buttons, dried beans, pasta pieces, paper clips, etc. all work well. You can also use "edible" manipulatives such as, dried cereal, pretzels, oyster crackers, small candies, raisins, banana chips, etc. (Make sure the children's hands and desk tops are clean before using manipulatives that can be eaten.)

Muffin Tin Count - Have children count small objects out into a muffin tin. Example: "Place one peanut in each cup, now place two peanuts in each cup." By using paper baking cups, you can draw dots on the bottom of each paper cup and have the student count the number of dots and place that same number of items inside. As students begin to recognize their numbers, write the numerals on the bottom of the paper cups. (Egg cartons also work quite well.)

Count and String - Give each child a long shoelace knotted at one end. Encourage the children to count out a given number of large buttons and string them on their shoelace.

Handful Counting - Place a large number of manipulatives in a paper sack. Have the children take turns reaching in with one hand and grabbing as many as they can. Help the child count out the number in his or her hand. Replace the manipulatives in the sack for the next student. Cotton balls, cut pieces of sponge, unshelled nuts, etc. all work well.

Counting Cards - Cut ten to twenty pieces of poster board measuring 8 1/2" X11". Glue cotton balls to each card with card one having one cotton ball, card two, two cotton balls, and so on. Write the appropriate number on the back of each card. Have the child feel and count the cotton balls and turn over the card to see the correct (numeral) number.

Toss and Count - Have students toss bean bags into a box or basket as they count them. You can also have them count how many times they toss a ball as you play catch.

Food Count - Help each youngster spread peanut butter or cream cheese onto a saltine cracker or stalk of celery and then count out a given number of raisins to place on top before eating.. (Frosting on a graham cracker with small candies or nuts, works well also.)

Number Count - Cut a large-sized number from heavy paper for each child in class. Provide small white glue bottles and numerous small objects (beans, macaroni, rubber bands, paper clips, etc.) Instruct each child to glue the appropriate number of each item to the cut-out number. Display the numbers in sequence on the class board.

Countdown Orders - Get children to obey at the same time you reinforce counting in sequence. Here are some ideas:

> Be quiet before I count to ten.
> Put on your shoes before I count from ten to twenty.
> Drink your milk before I count backwards from ten to one.
> Pick up your toys before I count by tens to one hundred.

Note: It's also fun to ask children to do silly things like; "Bend down and touch your toes before I count to five!"

Other Ways to Count - Have children count the following:

fingers and toes	spoons in the kitchen drawer
button on their shirts	towels in the cupboard
bounces of a ball	books on a shelf
number of kids with brown hair	number of claps
toys as they put them away	number of pockets
number of windows in a room	cookies in a bag
rings of a telephone	coins in your pocket (pennies, nickels, etc.)
number of yellow cars they see on the road	steps as they go up and down stairs

NUMBER IDEAS:

Sidewalk Numbers - Draw the numbers 1-10 or 1-20 on the sidewalk with chalk. Have students jump in order as they count. You can also ask students to, "Jump to number 6. Or, "Jump two jumps and tell me what number you are on." Let the child give you directions and you do the jumping!

Number Find - Write the numbers on large sheets of construction paper. (One number to each sheet. Place the numbered papers at random on the floor. Ask each child to "Point to the 4." Or, "Touch the 6 with your toe."

Numbering Fingers - Have each child place his or hand on a piece of construction paper and trace around it with a felt-tip marker. Help the child count the number of fingers on the tracing. Write the corresponding numerals on the fingers of the tracing and encourage the child to use it for number practice.

Number Lines - Post a number line (1-20) in your classroom. Use a purchased number line or make one yourself. Make sure that the numbers are written in clear, standard format and can easily be seen across the room. You could also post the number words, as well.

Sandpaper Numbers - Cut numbers from sandpaper and glue them to a larger sheet of poster board. Have each child trace the number with his or her finger. Instruct children to place a sheet of paper on top of the number and color over it with a crayon to make a number rubbing.

Creative Numerals - Try some of these ways to have kids make and practice their numbers. Start out with a large, written number on a piece of construction paper.

- Give the child a small bottle of white glue and piece of yarn. Help him glue the yarn over the one you have written on the paper.
- Have the child place colorful stickers on the written number.
- Give the child a rubber stamp and stamp pad. Help him stamp designs along the number.
- Help children glue small objects following the shape of the number. Provide different objects for each number and post the number sheets on the class board. You can then ask the children to identify the numbers by saying, "Which number is the peanut number?"

NUMBER GAMES:

Try these simple games to help reinforce number recognition and counting:

Number Trace - On a child's back, trace a number and have him or her name the number. Let the child trace a number on your back as well and you do the guessing.

Number Thinking - Ask the children questions such as, "I'm thinking of a number that tells me how many buttons I have; I'm thinking of a number that tells me what time school starts; I'm thinking of a number between 3 and 5; I'm thinking of a number that tells me how old Joey is."

Number Circle - Ask the children to sit in a circle. Call out a number between 1-10. Explain to the children that the object of the game is to not say that number. Select one student to start and have each student around the circle count in numerical order. The child that has to state the chosen number must leave the circle and sit in the middle. The game continues with the next child starting the countdown again with number one. Continue the game until only one child remains in the circle.

WORKSHEET IDEAS:

The worksheets in this book can also be used to make patterns and additional activities. Here are a few ideas:

Number Books - Have each child make their own number books as each number is introduced. The worksheets can be included in each book along with student-made number pages.

Matching Numbers - Copy the worksheets onto colored index paper. Laminate the pages and cut them apart for students to use as number matching activities.

Wipe-Off Worksheets - Copy the worksheets onto index paper and laminate them to provide a reusable surface. Have students take turns doing the activities using dark colored crayons. Show them how to erase the marks by using a dry paper towel.

WRITING NUMBERS:

Have children use "rainbow writing" when first learning to trace and write numbers. "Rainbow Writing" is when students use several different colors of crayons to trace each number.

I know my numbers!

☐ 1 to 10   ☐ 1 to 20

_____
Name

_____   _____
Teacher   Date

I can count to ___!

_____
Name

_____   _____
Teacher   Date

Group _____

123
Number Skills
Check List!

Names

Match One to One										
Count to 3										
Count to 5										
Count to 10										
Count to 15										
Count to 20										
Sort and Compare Objects										
Trace and Write Numbers 1-10										
Trace and Write Numbers 1-20										
Understand the Meaning of Zero										
Can Estimate										
Can Identify Patterns and Relationships										
Identifies Some Number Words										

Trace and write the number one.

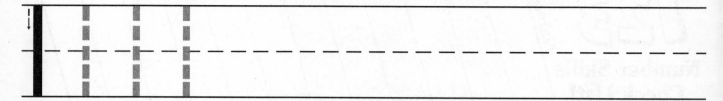

Color the number one.

Count to 1!

Trace and write the number two.

2 2 2 2 2

Color the number two.

Count to 2!

Trace and write the number three.

3 3 3 3

Color the number three.

Count to 3!

1 ———————————— 2 ———————————— 3

Color 3 pencils.

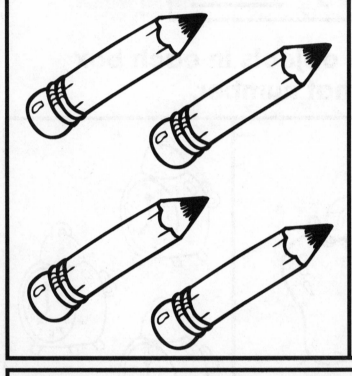

Color 3 scissors.

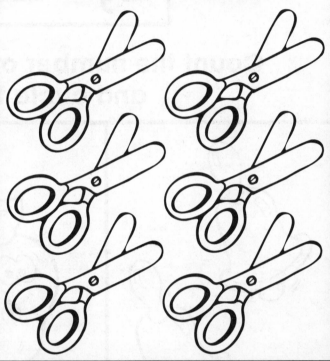

Draw a line to match the number to the correct number of objects.

2

1

3

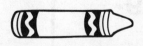
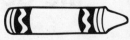

© Teacher's Friend, a Scholastic Company

TF1455 Little Kids...Count!

"I can count to 3!" Write the missing numeral.

1, 2, ____

Count the number of objects in each box and circle that number.

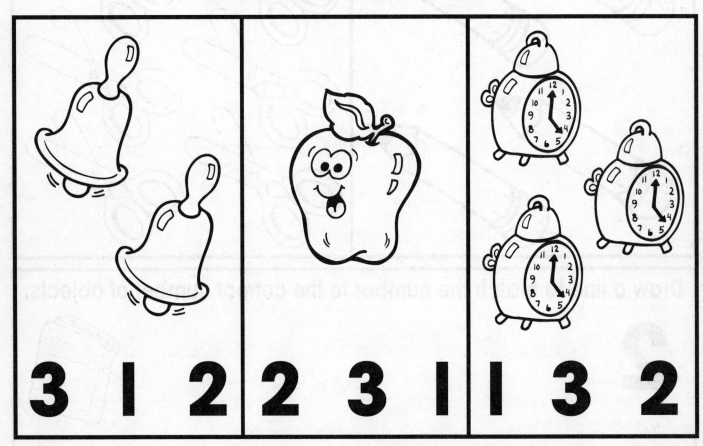

3 1 2   2 3 1   1 3 2

Draw 3 spots on the dog.

Trace and write the number four.

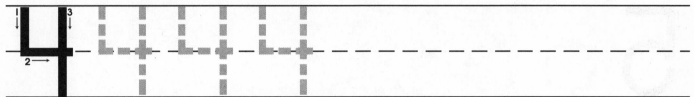

Color the number four.

Count to 4!

Trace and write the number five.

5 5 5 5 5

Color the number five.

Count to 5!

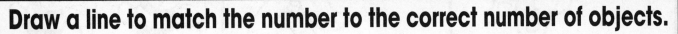

1   2   3   4   5

Color 5 butterflies.

Color 5 snails.

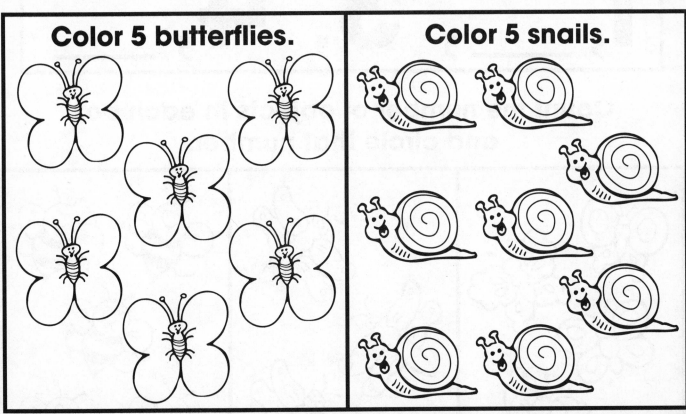

Draw a line to match the number to the correct number of objects.

4

5

3

"I can count to 5!" Write the missing numeral.

1, ___, 3, 4, ___

Count the number of objects in each box and circle that number.

4 5 3   2 4 3   5 2 3

Draw 5 bees around this beehive.

Trace and write the number six.

6 6 6 6

Color the number six.

Count to 6!

Trace and write the number seven.

Color the number seven.

Count to 7!

Trace and write the number eight.

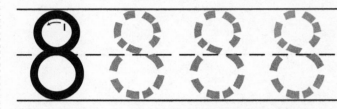

Color the number eight.

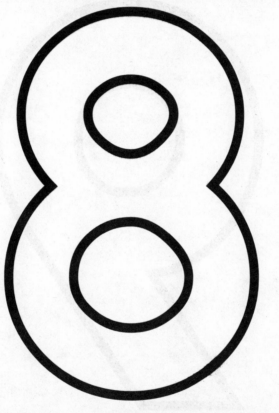

Count to 8!

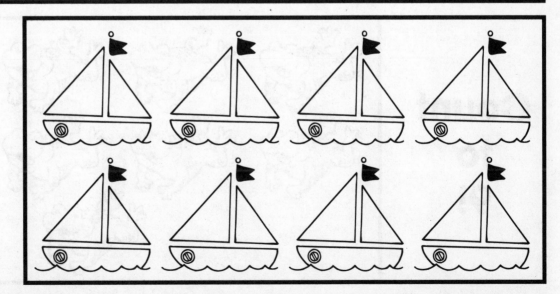

Trace and write the number nine.

9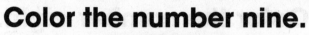

Color the number nine.

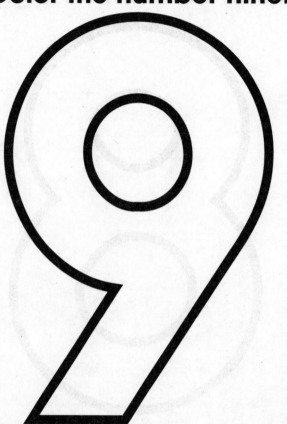

Count to 9!

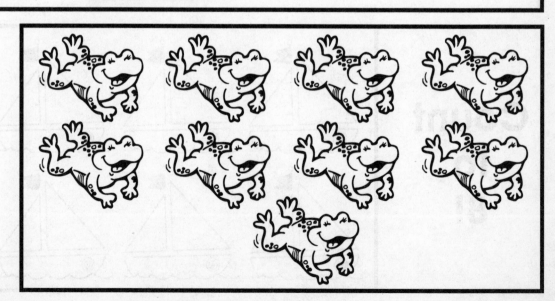

Trace and write the number ten.

10 10 10 10 10 10

Color the number ten.

Count to 10!

Color 10 fish.

Color 10 turtles.

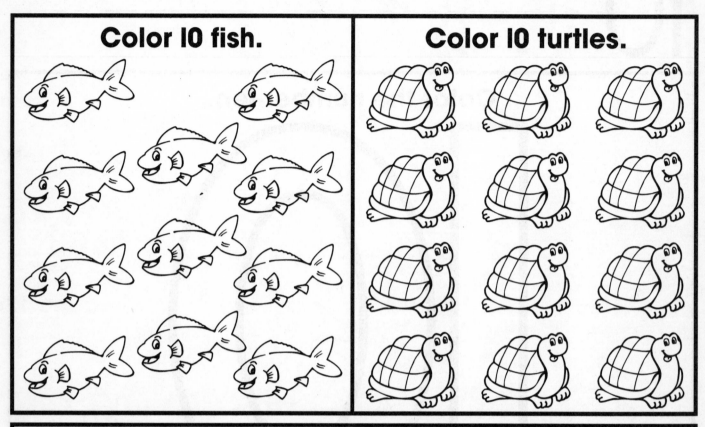

Draw a line to match the number to the correct number of objects.

10   8   9

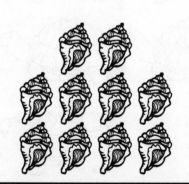

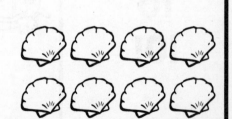

"I can count to 10!" Write the missing numeral.

1, 2, __, 4, 5, __, 7, 8, __, 10

Count the number of objects in each box and circle that number.

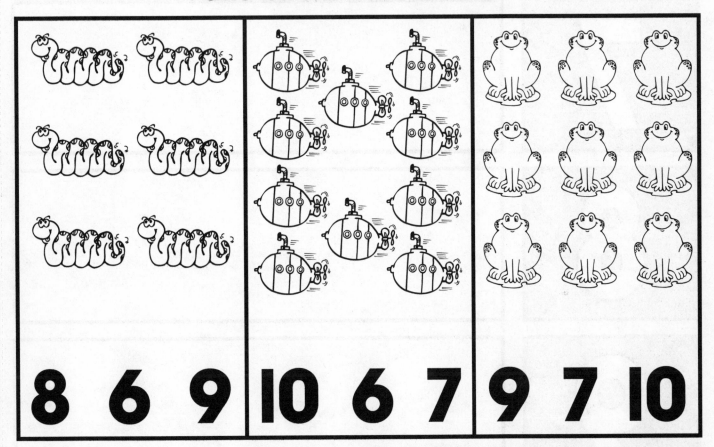

8   6   9   **10   6   7**   **9   7   10**

Draw 10 fish in the fish bowl.

Draw, stamp or glue the correct number of items in the box next to the number.

6	
7	
8	
9	
10	

Trace and write the number eleven.

Color the number eleven.

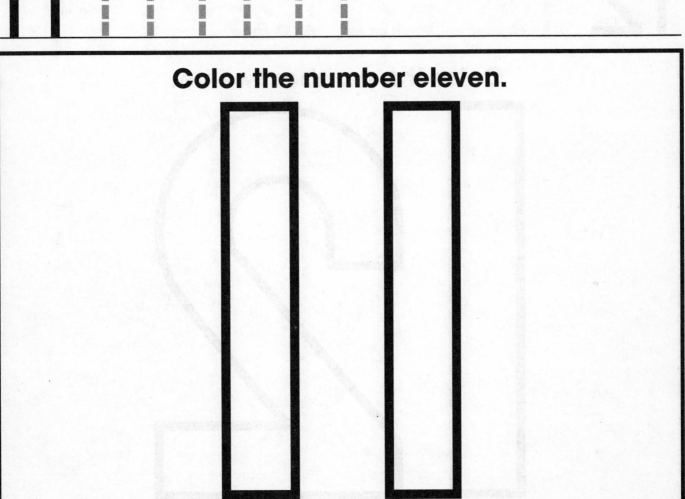

Count to 11!

Trace and write the number twelve.

12 12 12 12 12

Color the number twelve.

Count to 12!

Trace and write the number thirteen.

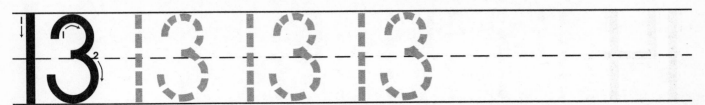

Color the number thirteen.

Count to 13!

Trace and write the number fourteen.

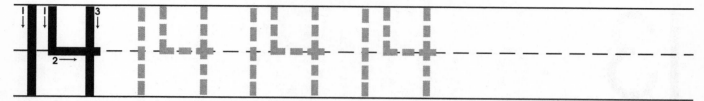

Color the number fourteen.

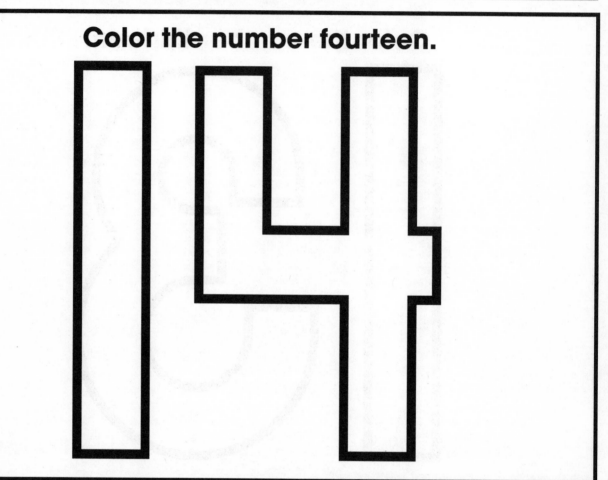

Count to 14!

Trace and write the number fifteen.

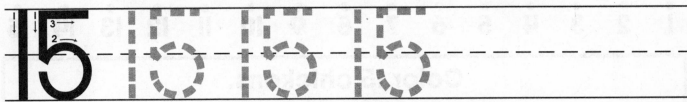

Color the number fifteen.

Count to 15!

"I can count to 15!"

1 2 3 4 5 6 7 8 9 10 11 12 13 14 15

Color 15 chickens.

Draw a line to match the number to the correct number of objects.

12　　　15　　　13

"I can count to 15!" Write the missing numeral.

9, ___, 11, 12, ___, 14, ___

Count the number of objects in each box and circle that number.

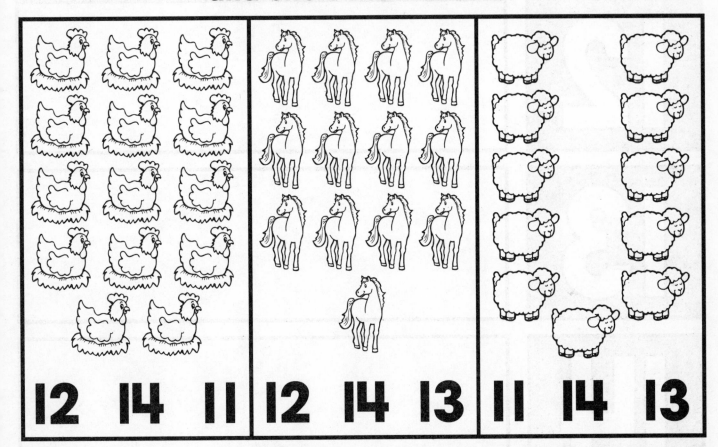

| 12 | 14 | 11 | 12 | 14 | 13 | 11 | 14 | 13 |

Draw 15 apples on the apple tree.

Draw, stamp or glue the correct number of items in the box next to the number.

11	
12	
13	
14	
15	

Trace and write the number sixteen.

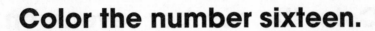

Color the number sixteen.

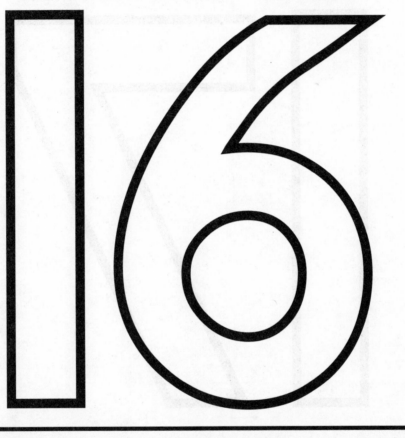

Count to 16!

Trace and write the number seventeen.

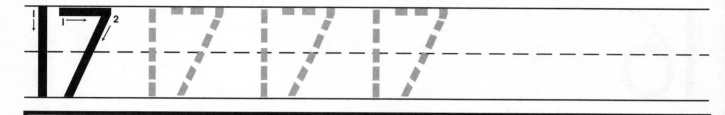

Color the number seventeen.

Count to 17!

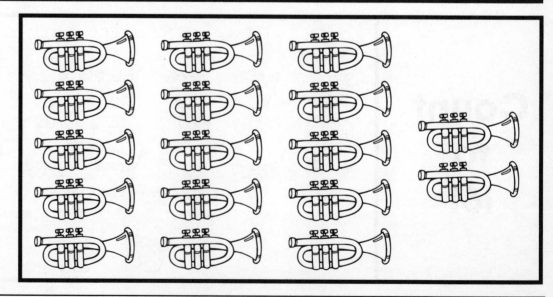

Trace and write the number eighteen.

18 18 18 18 18

Color the number eighteen.

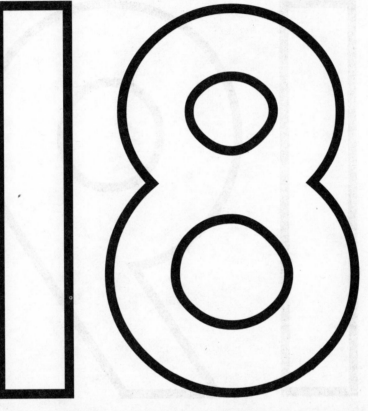

Count to 18!

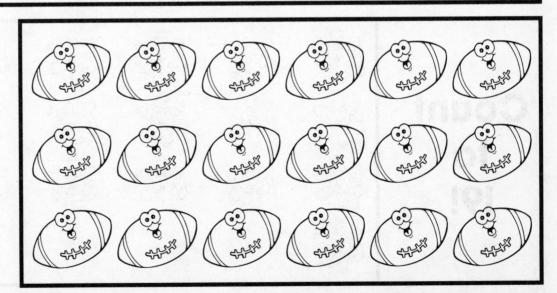

© Teacher's Friend, a Scholastic Company

Trace and write the number nineteen.

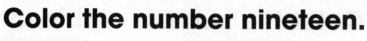

Color the number nineteen.

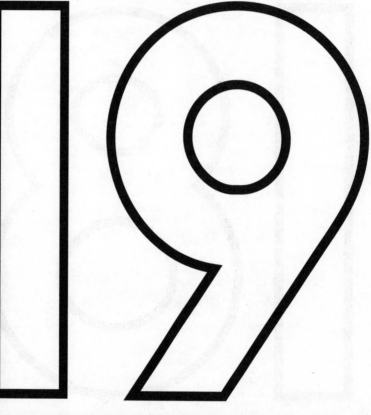

Count to 19!

Trace and write the number twenty.

20 20 20

Color the number twenty.

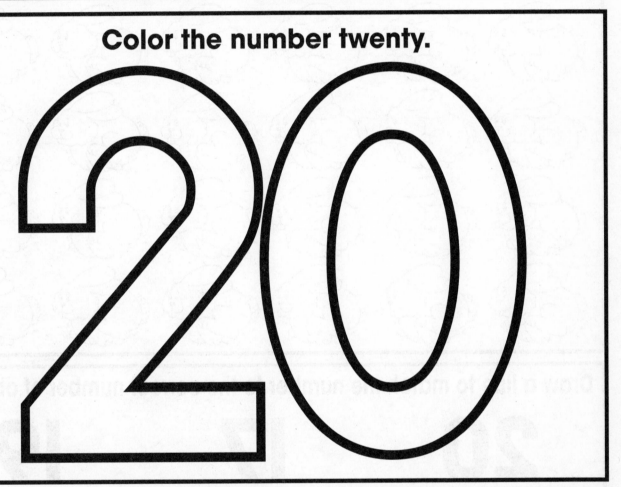

Count to 20!

"I can count to 20!"

1 2 3 4 5 6 7 8 9 10 11 12 13 14 15 16 17 18 19 20

Color 20 bunnies.

Draw a line to match the number to the correct number of objects.

20   17   19

 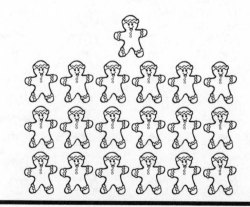

"I can count to 20!" Write the missing numeral.

15, 16, ___, ___, 19, ___

Count the number of objects in each box and circle that number.

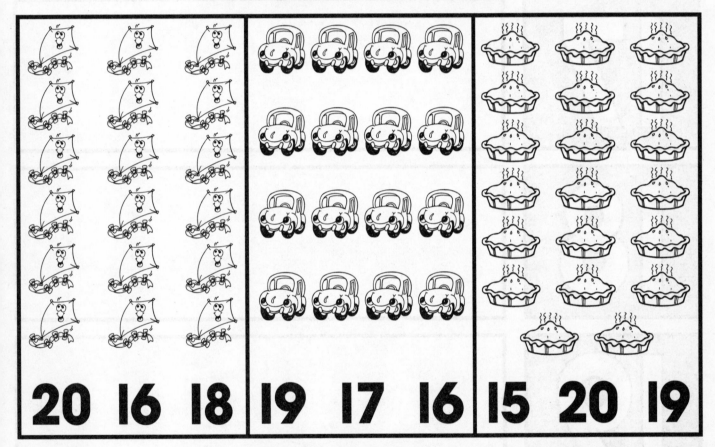

| 20 | 16 | 18 | 19 | 17 | 16 | 15 | 20 | 19 |

Draw 20 stars.

© Teacher's Friend, a Scholastic Company

TF1455 Little Kids...Count!

Draw, stamp or glue the correct number of items in the box next to the number.

16	
17	
18	
19	
20	

My Counting Wheel!

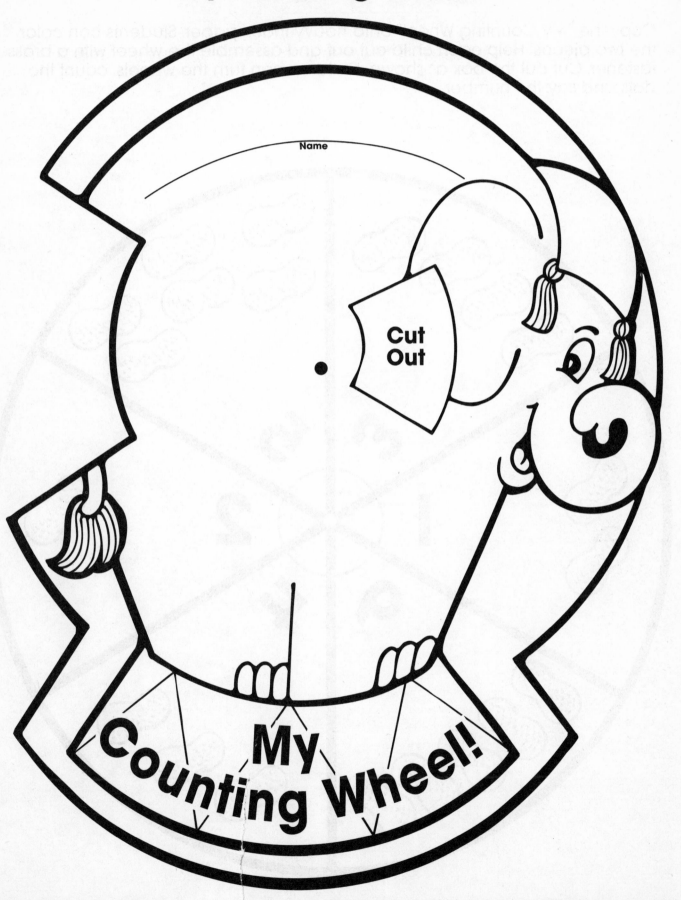

Name

Cut Out

My Counting Wheel!

My Counting Wheel!

Copy the "My Counting Wheel" onto heavy index paper. Students can color the two pieces. Help each child cut out and assemble the wheel with a brass fastener. Cut out the box as shown. Children can turn the wheels, count the dots and say the number.

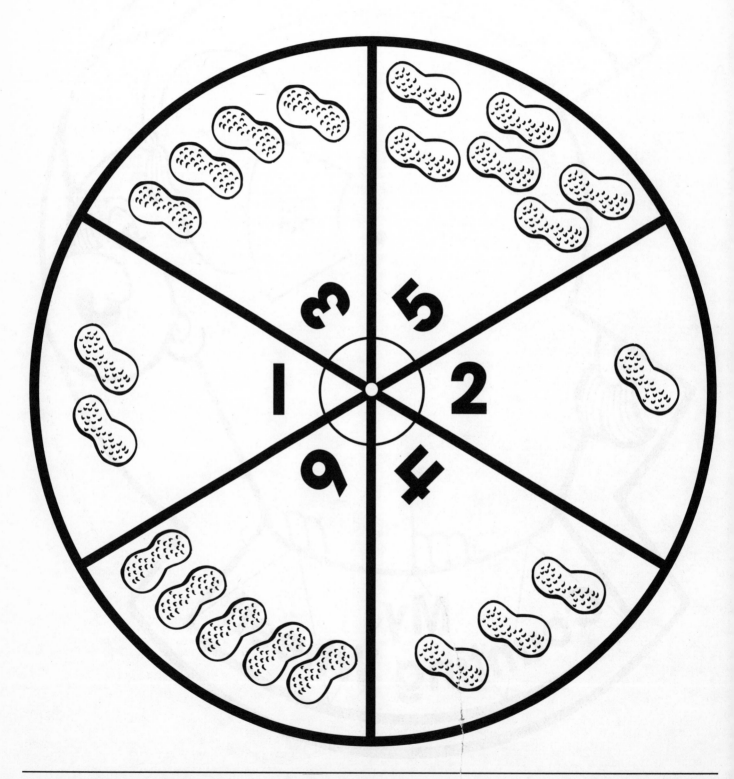

My Counting Wheel!

Cut Out

My
Counting
Wheel!

Name

© Teacher's Friend, a Scholastic Company

TF1455 Little Kids...Count!

My Counting Wheel!

Copy the "My Counting Wheel" onto heavy index paper. Students can color the two pieces. Help each child cut out and assemble the wheel with a brass fastener. Cut out the box as shown. Children can turn the wheels, count the dots and say the number.

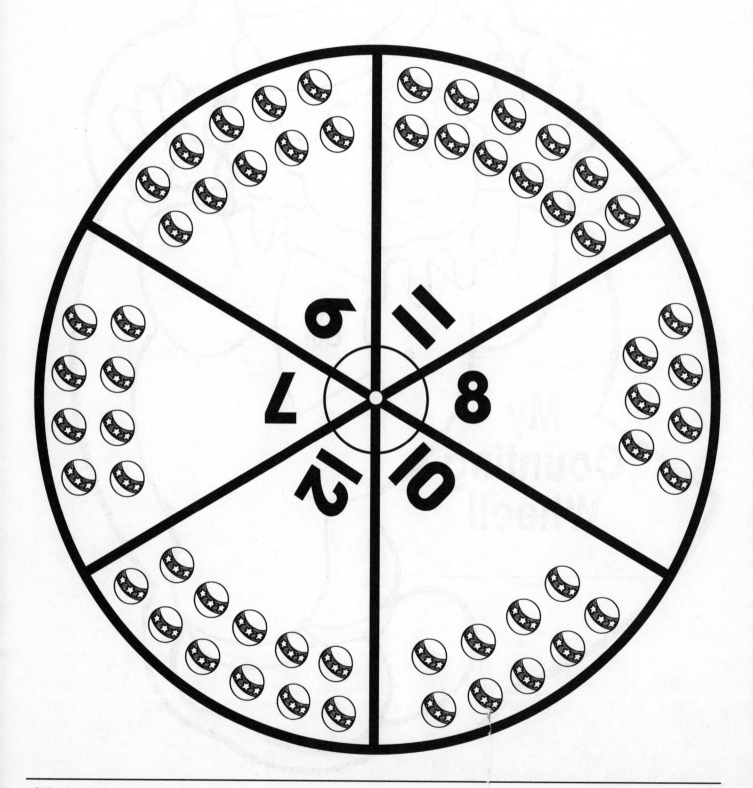

Count and Paste 1-6

Cut out the numbers at the bottom of the page. Count each group of objects and paste the correct number in the box.

Count and Paste 7-12

Cut out the numbers at the bottom of the page. Count each group of objects and paste the correct number in the box.

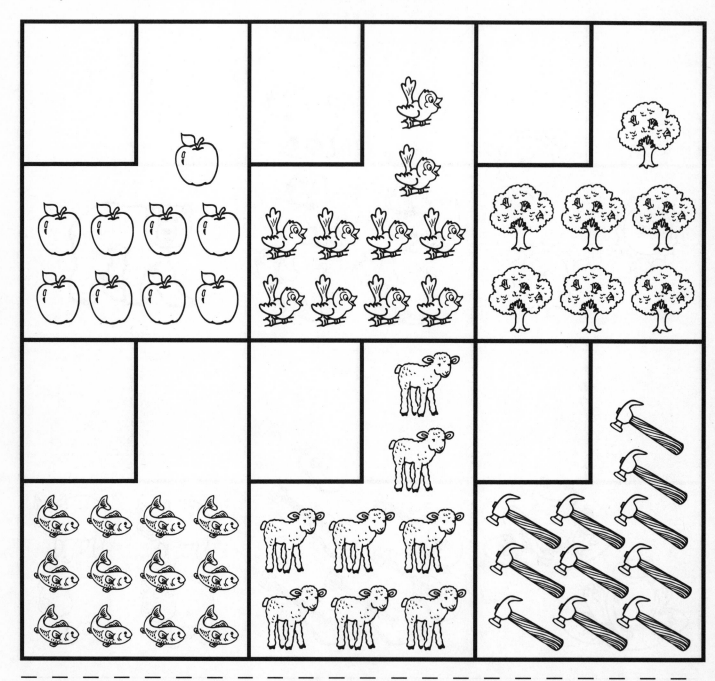

Trace these number words.

1 one

2 two

3 three

4 four

5 five

© Teacher's Friend, a Scholastic Company

TF1455 Little Kids...Count!

Trace these number words.

6 six

7 seven

8 eight

9 nine

10 ten

© Teacher's Friend, a Scholastic Company

48